D0583678

EDGE BOOKS

Into the Great Outdoors

Pheasant Hunting For Kids

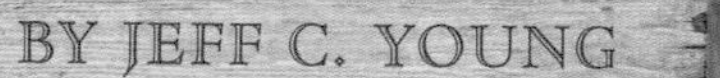

Consultant:
Rehan Nana
Pheasants Forever, Inc. and Quail Forever
St. Paul, Minnesota

CAPSTONE PRESS
a capstone imprint

Edge Books are published by Capstone Press,
1710 Roe Crest Drive, North Mankato, Minnesota 56003
www.capstonepub.com

Library of Congress Cataloging-in-Publication Data
Young, Jeff C., 1948-
Pheasant hunting for kids / by Jeff C. Young.
p. cm. – (Edge books. Into the great outdoors)
Includes bibliographical references and index.
ISBN 978-1-4296-9900-6 (library binding)
ISBN 978-1-62065-696-9 (paperback)
ISBN 978-1-4765-1555-7 (ebook PDF)
1. Pheasant shooting—Juvenile literature. I. Title.
SK325.P5Y68 2013
799.2′4625—dc23 2012022630

Editorial Credits
Brenda Haugen, editor; Gene Bentdahl, designer; Eric Gohl, media researcher; Kathy McColley, production specialist

Photo Credits
AP Images: Ames Tribune/ Nirmalnedu Majumdar, 25, Douglas C. Pizac, 20, Garden City Telegram/Rachael Gray, 11, Hays Daily News/Fred Hunt, 17; Capstone Studio: Karon Dubke, 23; Corbis: Heritage Images, 4, Peter Beck, 28–29; iStockphotos: Jason Lugo, 19; Newscom: MCT/Duluth News Tribune/ Sam Cook, 8–9; Shutterstock: Borislav Borisov, 3, Glenkar, 26–27, Lars Kastilan, 14, Linn Currie, 13, Reddogs, 6, Robynrg, cover, Tom Reichner, 1

The author dedicates this book to his pheasant hunting cousin, Terry W. Hanna.

Printed in the United States of America in Brainerd, Minnesota.
092012 006938BANGS13

TABLE OF CONTENTS

CHAPTER 1

BAGGING A BIRD

Your hunting dog has found a bunch of pheasants and scared them out of their hiding places. Your heart beats faster as you see the frightened birds flying through the air. You pick one bird as your target and carefully aim your shotgun. Bang! You've bagged your first pheasant.

History

Pheasants were first imported to the British colonies in North America in the 1700s. President George Washington had pheasants sent to his Mount Vernon, Virginia, home. The colonial governors of New Hampshire and New York also imported pheasants. But most of those birds were not hardy enough to survive.

The first successful attempt to bring pheasants to America was in 1881. About 24 ring-necked pheasants were imported from China. The birds were released in the Willamette Valley in Oregon. The pheasants thrived in their new home. In 1892 Oregon opened a 75-day pheasant hunting season.

In the early 1900s, other states and parts of Canada began importing pheasants. The small farms and rows of trees and shrubs found during that time were the perfect **habitat** for the birds. The pheasant population quickly grew, and hunting pheasants became a popular activity.

habitat—the natural place and conditions in which an animal or plant lives

During the 1970s and 1980s, many small farms were replaced by larger farms. The trees and shrubs where pheasants nested were often removed. Chemicals used to kill weeds and insects reduced the pheasants' food sources. The pheasant population began to decrease.

A U.S. government program called the **Conservation** Reserve Program (CRP) helped the pheasant population. The CRP paid small farmers to set aside pieces of land where crops would not be raised. The program also paid farmers for planting grasses that provided cover for pheasants.

Today there are millions of pheasants in North America. The birds can now be hunted without fear of a serious population decrease.

ring-necked rooster pheasant

Breeds

About 35 **species** of pheasants live in North America. Of those species, the ring-necked pheasant is the most common.

Male pheasants are called roosters. Roosters are usually 30 to 36 inches (76 to 91 centimeters) long. Each rooster has black, brown, blue, gray, and gold feathers. It also has a white ring around its neck.

Female pheasants are called hens. Hens are smaller than roosters, and their feathers aren't as brightly colored. Hens are mostly tan with dark spots on their feathers.

FACT

Roosters attract mates by crowing. They make raspy "kaw kaw" calls about every three minutes. Roosters also attract hens by strutting around with their feathers ruffled and their wattles swollen.

conservation—the protection of animals and plants, as well as the wise use of what we get from nature

species—a group of animals or plants that share common characteristics

wattle—the fleshy lobe found around the eye of a pheasant

CHAPTER 2
GEAR AND
HUNTING DOGS

Pheasant hunting takes some planning. You need to be properly outfitted before you begin the hunt. A little preparation and the right gear can help make your hunting trip a success.

Clothing

The clothing you wear for hunting needs to keep you dry and warm. Avoid cotton clothing because it retains moisture. Dress in layers so you can remove or add clothing as the temperature changes.

You will likely walk through some difficult terrain as you hunt pheasants. Hunters often wear an outside layer of nylon, such as a nylon jacket. Nylon clothing helps keep thorns and burrs from sticking to your clothes and cutting your skin. To protect their legs, hunters often wear brush pants or field chaps. You will also need a pair of sturdy boots to protect your feet.

Shotguns

Shotguns are used to hunt pheasants. When choosing a shotgun, pick one that is light enough for you to carry for a long time. You may be walking for a while when searching for pheasants. Carrying a heavy gun can tire your arms and make your shot unsteady.

Shotguns have different gauges. The gauge is the width of a shotgun's **barrel**. Guns with lower gauges are more powerful than higher-gauge guns. The most common gauges used in pheasant hunting are 12, 16, and 20.

Most pheasant hunters use shotguns with barrels that are 26 to 30 inches (66 to 76 cm) long. Some hunters prefer using short-barreled guns because they are easier to carry and shoot than long-barreled guns.

barrel—the long, tube-shaped metal part of a gun through which bullets or pellets travel

FACT

Pheasants can fly much faster than humans can run. Normally pheasants fly between 27 and 38 miles (43 and 61 km) per hour. When they are chased, the birds can reach speeds of up to 60 miles (97 km) per hour.

Hunting Dogs

Hunters who use trained dogs to track and **flush** out pheasants are able find and shoot more birds. Dogs have a much better sense of smell than people do. Hunting dogs are able to easily pick up the scent of nearby pheasants. Dogs called pointers signal to hunters when birds are nearby. Other dogs called flushers run toward the birds to get them to flee. This method gives a hunter a clear shot at the birds as they fly away.

Hunting dogs are also used to retrieve pheasants after the birds have been shot. The dogs find where the birds have fallen and keep wounded birds from getting away.

flush—to drive an animal from its hiding place

golden retriever

FACT
The breeds most often used for pheasant hunting include Labrador retrievers, English springer spaniels, golden retrievers, German shorthaired pointers, and Brittanys.

CHAPTER 3

TIPS AND TECHNIQUES

Before you bag a pheasant, you must know where and when you can hunt them. Pheasant hunting laws vary by state. States also set hunting seasons. It's against the law to hunt pheasants out of season or to trespass on private property to hunt. Obeying hunting laws keeps the sport safe and fun for everyone.

Seasons and Licensing

In most states, pheasant-hunting season begins in October. It usually lasts from three to 10 weeks, depending on the area's pheasant population.

Each hunter must purchase a license before hunting pheasants. The minimum age for buying a hunting license varies from state to state. In some states, hunters as young as 13 years old can get licenses as long as they follow added rules. Usually they need to take an approved hunter education and firearms safety class before getting a license. They also have to hunt with an adult who has a hunting license. You can find out the laws in your state by contacting your local conservation office.

SNOW HUNTING

During snowy weather, pheasants are usually grouped in a smaller area. Snowy conditions limit their feeding areas and places to hide. And like many other wild animals, pheasants seek shelter when it snows. Look for places where pheasants might seek shelter. You can also follow their tracks.

Fresh snow on the ground makes it easier to find pheasant tracks. At other times, tracking is harder because pheasant tracks in dirt and mud are covered by grass. Experienced trackers can even tell the difference between hen tracks and rooster tracks. A rooster's tail usually leaves a drag mark in the snow. If you plan to track pheasants, do so right after it snows. Otherwise you won't know how old the tracks are, and the pheasants may already be gone.

Finding Pheasants

You will find pheasants in different places depending on the time of day you hunt. Pheasants often stay in areas close to a food supply. Shortly after sunrise, pheasants leave their **roosting cover** to eat. Usually their feeding area is a field that provides food and tall grasses that make the birds harder to see. Areas with ragweed, soybeans, corn, and other small grains are popular feeding spots. Pheasants eat for an hour or two before returning to their roosting cover or **loafing cover**. Their loafing cover is usually a grassy area close to the food source.

About an hour before sundown, pheasants go out for a second feeding. After they've eaten again, they settle into their roosting cover for the night.

FACT

You may also find pheasants on wetlands, fence lines or ditches, and undisturbed grassy fields. Any area that isn't regularly mowed or plowed is a good place to look.

roosting cover—a place, such as a tree or brush, where pheasants spend the night

loafing cover—a place where pheasants go to rest during the middle part of the day

Drive Hunting

Pheasant hunters often drive hunt. Hunters form a line by standing closely together, side by side. These hunters are called drivers. The drivers slowly move toward another line of hunters at the other end of a field. The hunters in this second line are called blockers. As the drivers move toward the blockers, they frighten the pheasants in the field. Then the birds fly toward the blockers.

Before they start, the drivers and blockers decide which hunters will do the shooting. They also decide on the direction of their shots. This practice helps make sure that blockers and drivers won't be shooting toward one another.

Taking Your Shot

It's important to know the right time to shoot. If you shoot too soon, the bird will fly away and won't return. If you shoot a pheasant at close range, there won't be much left to clean and cook. If you wait too long, the bird may be out of your gun's range. You may then injure the bird instead of killing it. An injured bird is hard to retrieve because it can quickly fly or run away. Injuring birds instead of killing them also is considered unsportsmanlike. Be sure you always know the range of your shotgun.

When aiming at a pheasant, hold one hand behind the shotgun's trigger and your other hand beneath the **forestock**. Use the hand beneath the forestock to raise the gun barrel. Use your other hand to place the gun on your shoulder. Aim at a spot about 3 feet (0.9 m) in front of the pheasant. This technique is called leading. As you shoot, continue to move the gun barrel in the direction of the pheasant's flight path.

FACT

Pheasants rely on their sharp sense of hearing to warn them of approaching danger. If you slam a car door or yell at your dog, the birds will fly or run away.

After a successful shot, you need to remember where the bird landed. You should find every bird that you have shot. Leaving a dead bird behind is not sportsmanlike behavior.

Keep both eyes open when you shoot. Pheasants often fly to the left or the right. Keeping both eyes open gives you a better chance of seeing a hazard, such as a person or a hunting dog.

forestock—the gun part located underneath the back end of the barrel

CHAPTER 4 SAFETY

Pheasant hunting is a fun activity, but any activity involving guns has risks. Being safe at all times should be a hunter's biggest concern.

Education Courses

Most states require that first-time hunters take a hunter education course before being issued hunting licenses. The course is often offered by the state agency that enforces hunting laws. The course teaches gun safety, hunting **ethics**, and conservation.

In many states, pheasant hunters are required to wear blaze orange clothing. This clothing makes it easier for hunters to see one another.

FACT

States started offering hunting safety courses in 1949. Since then, more than 35 million people have taken the courses.

Be Prepared

Before the hunt begins, let someone know where you will be hunting and how long you will be gone. You may want to bring a compass in case you get lost. You should also pack a small survival kit. Include a cell phone, a first-aid kit, some rope, a waterproof fire-starting kit, a knife, and a blanket in your kit.

Even if it's legal for you to hunt alone, it's best to hunt with others. Each person in your hunting party should carry food and water. High-energy snacks such as granola and beef jerky are good choices. Carry at least 1 quart (0.95 liter) of drinking water for every 5 miles (8 kilometers) you plan to walk. If you're using hunting dogs, remember to bring water for them too.

Johnson & Johnson
First Aid Kit
Emergency
Blanket
• Reflects body heat back to the body
• Aluminized polyester
• Wind and waterproof
LIFELINE
LIFELINE
Waterproof Safety Matches
strike on box only
www.lifelinefirstaid.com
SAMSUNG
Millville
OATS & HONEY
CRUNCHY GRANOLA BARS
Millville
Sweet & Salty Nut
GRANOLA BAR
with Almonds

Gun Safety

At all times, remember to follow two important rules of gun safety. First, never aim your weapon at anything you don't intend to shoot. Second, always treat every gun as if it were loaded.

Until you begin hunting, your gun should be unloaded. Never enter a camp area, vehicle, or home carrying a loaded gun. Your gun's **safety** must stay in the on position until you're ready to fire at your target.

Before you shoot, make sure that no one is standing between you and your target. You must also be aware of the area beyond your target. Make sure the area behind your target is clear so you don't accidentally shoot another person or animal.

safety—a device that prevents a gun from firing

FACT

Experts say you should never rely on your gun's safety. A safety can sometimes fail to work properly. Always handle your gun in a safe way, even if the safety is on.

CHAPTER 5 CONSERVATION

Nearly 2 million people hunt pheasants in the United States. By respecting the environment and following the rules, hunters make sure their sport can be enjoyed for years to come.

Hunting Conservation

Hunting out of season and bagging more pheasants than laws allow reduce the pheasant population. Hunters also should avoid shooting at pheasants that are too close together or that are out of the range of their weapons. These practices can wound pheasants and are considered unsportsmanlike.

Hunters also should help keep the environment clean. Don't leave litter behind. Also try to collect your empty shell casings whenever possible.

FACT

Hunting claims about half of the male pheasant population in the United States each hunting season.

Organizations

The efforts of conservation and hunting organizations have helped maintain North America's pheasant population. Pheasants Forever is the largest group in the United States and Canada devoted to protecting pheasants. The group has more than 135,000 members. Pheasants Forever works to protect and increase the populations of pheasants. The group's efforts include habitat improvements and education.

By becoming involved in conservation and hunting organizations, you can help secure the future of pheasant hunting. You can find out more about these organizations by contacting your state Department of Natural Resources or your local conservation office.

GLOSSARY

barrel (BAYR-uhl)—the long, tube-shaped metal part of a gun through which bullets or pellets travel

conservation (kon-sur-VAY-shuhn)—the protection of animals and plants, as well as the wise use of what we get from nature

ethics (ETH-iks)—having to do with right and wrong behavior

flush (FLUSH)—to drive an animal from its hiding place

forestock (FOR-stahk)—the gun part located underneath the back end of the barrel

habitat (HAB-uh-tat)—the natural place and conditions in which an animal or plant lives

loafing cover (LOH-fing KUHV-ur)—a place where pheasants go to rest during the middle part of the day; usually a grassy area

roosting cover (ROO-sting KUHV-ur)—a place, such as a tree or brush, where pheasants spend the night

safety (SAYF-tee)—a device that prevents a gun from firing

species (SPEE-sheez)—a group of animals or plants that share common characteristics

wattle (WAH-tuhl)—the fleshy lobe found around the eye of a pheasant

READ MORE

Carpenter, Tom. *Upland Bird Hunting: Wild Turkey, Pheasant, Grouse, Quail, and More.* Great Outdoors Sports Zone. Minneapolis: Lerner Publications Co., 2013.

Omoth, Tyler. *Turkey Hunting for Kids.* Into the Great Outdoors. North Mankato, Minn.: Capstone Press, 2013.

Pound, Blake. *Pheasant Hunting.* Outdoor Adventures. Minneapolis: Bellwether Media, Inc., 2013.

INTERNET SITES

FactHound offers a safe, fun way to find Internet sites related to this book. All of the sites on FactHound have been researched by our staff.

Here's all you do:

Visit *www.facthound.com*

Type in this code: 9781429699006

INDEX